The Voices of Women

poems by

Isabella David McCaffrey

Finishing Line Press
Georgetown, Kentucky

The Voices of Women

Copyright © 2016 by Isabella David McCaffrey
ISBN 978-1-944251-82-6 First Edition
All rights reserved under International and Pan-American Copyright Conventions. No part of this book may be reproduced in any manner whatsoever without written permission from the publisher, except in the case of brief quotations embodied in critical articles and reviews.

ACKNOWLEDGMENTS

These poems first appeared in the following publications:

Contemporary Haibun Online: "The Diviner" as "Hexagram 54 of the I Ching;" "The Vacationer" as "Lake-Watching"
Slippery Elm: "The Daughter" as "Rolling Stone Papa"
Adbusters: "The Girl in the Taxi" as "Taxi Ride"
Apollo's Lyre: "The Dreamer" as "A Dream Voluptuous and Sincere"
Postcard Poems & Prose, "The Bohemian"
Every Day Poets: "The Shopaholic" as "Project Shopaholic;" "The Sister" as "Horizons;" "The Helicopter Mother" as "Potty Training Awareness;" "The Trophy Bride;" , "The Scientist Panics at San Casciano" as "Panic at San Casciano;" "The Hipster Loves," as "Love Impermanence"
Postcard Shorts, "The Student" as "Concerning a Lost Balloon"
Gyroscope Review: "The Book Club Devotee" and "After Happily Ever After"

16 of these poems in pamphlet version were shortlisted for the 2015 International Venture Award. Four other poems were recognized for merit in *Atlanta Review*'s 2015 International Poetry Prize: "The Doe, or Death by Canyon", "The Girl in the Ghetto Contemplates Life from Nowhere New Jersey", "The Manga Girl Imagines Her Creator", and "The Eternal Grandmother, or The Supreme Moment Is Now."

Editor: Christen Kincaid
Cover Art: Hadar Pitchon
Author Photo: Hadar Pitchon
Cover Design: Elizabeth Maines

Printed in the USA on acid-free paper.
Order online: www.finishinglinepress.com
　　　also available on amazon.com

Author inquiries and mail orders:
Finishing Line Press
P. O. Box 1626
Georgetown, Kentucky 40324
U. S. A.

Table of Contents

The Voices of Women 1
The Housewife 2
The Doe, or Death by Canyon 3
The Bohemian 4
The Vacationer: A Haibun 5
The Shopaholic 6
The Girl in the Taxi 7
The Trophy Bride 10
The Book Club Devotee 11
The Scientist Panics Walking at San Casciano 13
The Helicopter Mother 14
The Diviner, or Hexagram 54 of the I Ching: A Haibun 15
The Poet Updates Israfel 16
The Daughter 17
The Girl in the Ghetto Contemplates Life from Nowhere
    New Jersey. 19
The Manga Girl Imagines Her Creator 21
The Eternal Grandmother, or the Supreme Moment
    Is Now 23
The Dreamer 25
The Hipster Loves 26
The Student 28
The Historian 29
"La Sérieuse" Academic Lectures 31
The Sisters: A Haibun 32
After Happily Ever After 33

For Ryan, Harper, and Moses-to-Be

"The sweetest of all sounds is that of the voice of the woman we love."
JEAN DE LA BRUYERE

The Voices of Women

The voices of women. Thin and high.
I imagine them as violin strings played
by a slightly mad musician
across all the dusks of the world, haunting me.

Or they are tender and crooning as Benedictine nuns.
They sing of children and blood together.
Of the mystery of the body.
Laudes antiquae of the trinity,
the moon, the tides, and all mysteries,
which women have no choice but to

contemplate, as autumn and spring
force us to feel the passion of scarlet, the tragedy of green,
to note how leaves and petals come and go, to dream
of circularity, eternity, and, always, of our need to touch

as voices chanting foreign words touch so easily the heart.

Or they murmur rhythmically, soft like
meditative breaths, hardly discernible,
unless, like a scientist, one listens with calculating

instruments to these butterfly
voices—*ave maria, ave*—small and fragile,
fluttering at the edges of
history, alighting for gathered seconds upon

sere leaves, quivering at every gust
of breeze and zephyr, blown away into the
wilderness of the night. Oh hush. Oh hush.

There is the holy lip of sky to kiss the stars.
Between the edges of things, the music comes.

The Housewife

Some women stay in the
stone house
for days
with the apple blossoms
falling all around
their bare toes in private gardens.

Before I can tell you
what I mean,
I have to tell you
about these women:

women who paint the
faces of the sky,
women who bear their young
and cry over thighs spreading
and bubbling like butter in a hot pan,
women who count strands of silver
like rings around tree trunks,
women whose eyes are limpid
pools of life and hope
like the sun and moon united
in one face.

Some women stay in the stone
house and the painted house
for days, feeding their young like
patient birds and never cutting
their wrists, no matter how tempting
the urge to flee becomes.

Like Simone Weil, they think they are
starving for God and man's sake.
Like Simone Weil, some women
suspect they are saints.

The Doe, or Death by Canyon

People walk around scattering the stars of their eyes
like little flower girls scattering blossoms from baskets.

They don't CGI the light out of actors' eyes, although
they could; I saw a deer die once on the side of the road,

and when the light faded from the iris without the pupil
so much as dilating, I knew she was gone.

That deer hit us, shot like an arrow out of the guerilla night
on a lone stretch of highway beside the canyon.

Between desert and abyss, it splattered across our windshield,
the surprised face for a millisecond fused to my own.

We pulled over and watched it die, toeing the dust,
not knowing what else to do under the desert stars.

I tried to say the Lord's Prayer, but being a Jew
couldn't remember it & the boy I was with despised

sentimentality. "Aw, c'mon," he said, cutting off my confusion
neatly. "Let's go!" But I wanted to wait, for what?

That ounce of soul to take flight and fling itself heavenward.
I do swear I saw the dark angel bend over her quieting muzzle,

gathering the light as humble janitors after the vow, the blessing,
the ring sweep up the remains of those fallen, withered roses.

The Bohemian

Orion is above us. I pluck the evening flower.
We are so poor—we are only here an hour.
We are so poor—we have always been with you
and Orion above us.

The grapes are sweet and the pears are heavy
in the dreams of the rich and in the woes of the poor.
We have no drink, no meat—I have a wreath of flowers.

I have the weight of hours.

The Vacationer: A Haibun

All day we watch gray clouds wash over the lake. Thunder like furniture being moved in the attic. Sunshowers that sprinkle sunlight and raindrops, and a storm thudding in with the North wind, causing us to rush, panicked to shut windows.

Later, a barge crosses the lake in stately slowness just as clouds part, and the sun sets. I see a tall, black silhouette against the rosy light and think of the Greeks dreaming of the afterlife, and I think once some ancient poet saw a ferryman during such a sunset as this, and Lethe was born. There's a throbbing in my heart and a kind of peace as I watch the distant figure on the boat, facing away towards a far, misty shore.

> pines grow on rocks, roots
> clinging to hardness that they
> may lap clear springs

The Shopaholic

Pin-tuck, pleat my dreams,
quilt me, hem me,
fully line my being
with purple-striped lambs wool

of only the highest quality.
Cut welt pockets through my cortex,
lay a white, lace inset in my soul,
sandblast vintage-inspired desires.

Fill the empty closet of my echoing skull
with the latest colors of the retail rainbow:
periwinkle, pumpkin, merlot. This season
my aura has a lean silhouette.

and back darts for shape,
so I always feel crisp and elegant.
My totem shall be zebra-printed
on a cardigan of super-fine, 12-gauge knit.

Hook my beliefs on a hood
that buttons or unbuttons,
depending on desired fit.
Most of all disguise, deform,

deplete my useless spirit
not worth a damn cent.
Don't let those others see
how unmarketable I can be.

The Girl in the Taxi

Those green desert-only eyes and skin baked red like clay and cracked like the dust under the sun,
looking at me from the rear-view mirror.
The cabdriver's eyes were oasis eyes.
His eyes were Wadi Rum in his old cracked dusty Egyptian cabdriver face.

He says: *It is in the ko'ran. Take care of your woman.*

I don't know anything anymore.
I don't know anything. Who cares?
Sometimes I look at tabloids I admit. I've gone soft.
I used to see the bodies in Africa and cry.

His eyes were fierce. The Egyptian cabdriver looking at me.

He says: *The prophet (allah akbar) said take care of your women.*
Three times they ask. Three times he say.
It is in the ko'ran. It is there in the ko'ran.

After I look at the tabloids I feel the way the desert felt to me that winter outside Cairo.
I was 18. It was my first broken heart.

His eyes were what my sister calls beautiful eyes. His eyes were the palest green.
They were shocking, they were so green, they were so pale, and there was a light in them. You could believe about the warriors in his past who went into Portugal. Who conquered Spain.

Who took, who raped, who ruled, who taught.

There aren't so many green things in a desert you can forget a pair of eyes like that.

He says: *A man who takes care of his women is a man who has no problems.*

When he says Ko'ran there is a glottal stop. He tells me unasked for about Empire and pain.

That's his truth. Mine is simpler these days. I find a lot of it in magazines. Sometimes I flip through the glossy pages and I don't see a single face
What I mean is there is hunger and there is hunger. There is a banality

that starves faces.

But who am I to say? Who am I to say anything?

He says: *First there is the love of the mother. There is no love like the love of the mother.*

Those everyday eyes of destitution. Those everyday eyes of disgrace. Those peony-powered eyes. Those cat-lined eyes. Those cool, calm collected eyes. Those eyes all around me. But I don't know why I'm so afraid. On the other
hand, I don't agree.

He says: *Then there is the sister. There is no love like the love of the sister.*

Those painted faces that no sky has ever rained upon and no sun has shone too hard on or done anything but illuminate and whose nostrils have never quivered except with distaste and whose ears have gone deaf to anything not burnable. But that could just be me.

Maybe that's unfair. Maybe I'm just afraid of death.

He says: *Then there is the love of the wife. And the daughter. This is love.* The old Egyptian cabdriver is crying. Only a little bit. It's strange. But I don't judge. I don't judge tears anyway. I cry enough tears. I heard that's good. I hope I'm not crazy. I hope he's not crazy.

He says: *This is love.*

He strikes the steering wheel. He strikes the steering wheel three times.

Three times with an open fist. He's crying, but he isn't sad.

There aren't a lot of tears. It's sentimentality, but it's not the sentimentality that shames you or exhorts you. It just is. He strikes the steering wheel again and clears his voice.

He says: *Whenever you need a kiss or hug, there is the mother, the sister, the wife, the daughter.*

He has a burned brown face. The wrinkles baked in much deeper than the New York sun can reach into anyone I see. Even the leathery shore ladies don't have a face like him.

He says: *This is love. This is true love. People don't understand true love.*

I look at tabloids too often. They make me cry. People don't understand. There is suffering and there is suffering. I'm not sure which is which. I'm not sure I should compare these things. Maybe it's all facts, after all. Maybe we poets worry too much.

Maybe we worry too much about being in love and feeling alive and having a soul.

Maybe that stuff doesn't matter. Maybe it doesn't matter like real hunger does. Maybe it matters more. I can only live this one life. I can only report what I see. I can only say how hungry I feel. I can only say how sad everyone seems.

He says: *A man who has this love has no problems.*

His eyes were very green. The Egyptian cabdriver who had no problems. I didn't say anything. I thought of Wadi Rum where it was green. Not in Egypt but near enough. He made me think of the desert I knew. And of the cool stream of water there. After we walked, we bathed.

I had my heart broken that year.

I used to lie awake in the desert and dream.

The Trophy Bride

They told me my prince would come,
and he did. I let his wealth bespeak
his love. He made me heavy, gold, his bride
bedecked from spangled nape of

neck to aurous tip of toe. I was
a neon sign of our romance and
how they stared when we danced
unwieldy at our wedding feast

like gypsies carrying upon our backs
all the worldly goods we had,
though ours were diamantine and rare.
We lumbered, shambled, clumped our way

through our *lune de miel* at Biarritz.
(You taught me to speak in French phrases,
my Midas, and I learned a trick or *deux*
for you, *mon amour*.)

They told me I would grow to love
your rapacious touch, your greedy caress,
but my coffered heart has turned as cold
as all the metals in your treasure chests.

The Book Club Devotee

We read the Pisan Cantos LXXIV-LXXXIV
aloud between surplus paper napkins and
folding metal chairs, squeezed into a corner
like some 12-step poetry group.

A circle of frail human beings
with bad haircuts and pilled sweaters,
taking turns with each stanza diffidently as if
on the verge of composing a love sonnet or
confessing to lifelong sins of flesh and spirit.

Deconstructing passages of sadistic,
opaque splendor, speaking in tongues
about fallen heroes, skipping the Chinese
altogether but admiring on the page the symbols
as exquisite as Tanagra figurines.

  "J'ai eu pitié des autres."
An old man reads, his Bronx
accent laying the vowels like underground subway
tracks deep inside his nostrils, sprouting white hair
and syllables.

He pushes his glasses up a beautifully bulbous nose,
pausing to squint:

  "Probablement pas assez."

No, never enough pity.
I'm thinking of Pound, mad and lonely and nostalgic.
I'm thinking of myself back then, young and loving poetry alone,
I'm thinking of the doomed days of the Poetry Club.
I'm thinking of the man reading French, never understanding a word

in the basement of the Bowery Poetry Club,
now replaced by another burlesque joint—
how the hip do inherit the Earth! And like locusts
will end by devouring us all.

  "Tard, très tard je t'ai connue la tristesse."

The air smelling of sadness and plumbing,
reading our happy doom
beneath a stark halo of fluorescent lights
in the basement of the Bowery Poetry Club
now a burlesque joint, serving up tits with $80 steaks.

And who's to say which is better? Breasts or odes to them.

"O so white, O so soft, O so sweet is she!"
Although never again will there be found such beautiful
talk of pity deep in the bowels and such hope to understand
handfuls of gathered words, illuminated by study and pain.

The Scientist Panics Walking at San Casciano

Passing the castle walls
as in a slow dream of early morning;
geraniums in blue state in cracked sills
and old donne in housedress
told me I was present and awake.
Where stone steps descended hot
to the valley in the sun I sat to peel an orange.
To a lost tourist said, *"Non so l'hora."*
Nor I did. A village like a medieval witch—
all cobweb shawl and thin cat, bells that cackled
Matins. Soon the steps became a slope I walked
past sulfur baths to pine grove's shadowy black.
Where shadow mixed silence deep with light
a shiver took me at my side the rustle
and then another and to the right and stillness
down the plain, so wild was the pause I ran.
And from this day I began
to believe, though silently, the dying Earth laughs long and hard
still, laughs at our human arrogance, scoffs at our creeds
with what it may: Pan some say, or dust, wind, and shadow.

The Helicopter Mother

"Baby's Latest: Going Diaperless." Such headlines mock my
pain, reading the paper to touch the world, but this image of
Madonna and child atop toilet cuts deep-- I only wish:
thoughts of trash we create torture me, undo my good:

eco-lightbulbs, old rags called vintage chic,
local strawberries in June and pomegranate seeds
in the fall like Persephone noshing through winter,
keeping basil simply to sustain green.

My baby is an angel who shits: there's no getting around it.
Her eyes look up at me with impossible trust;
I squeeze the diaper into a conical can, sealing smells
destined for the barge we daily contribute to, this unbenediction—

this rude, modern offering to the great gods of sky and water:
a ship bearing bottles, nappies,
old shoes, fat of lambs, lemon rinds to the salt sea
blasting back pale foam with the rising wind,

brandishing impotence like the lady of the lake,
who once offered Excalibur from unsullied waters, her white
sleeve signaling now total surrender as putrescent cargo is
unloaded onto the backs of whales and fish.

I settle baby, a bottle handy, gently rock her,
absently read the article describing bowel in bowl
collection—constant vigilance! A Monty Python sketch.
The ethos of "elimination communication."

A bandaid to contain gangrenous wounds we inflict on the Earth.
Will I hold her bare bottom between cars in the street?
Ay me! I will let my bowls and baby be separate by land,
mixed only and alone by the magic of the salty sea.

The Diviner, Or Hexagram 54 of the I Ching: A Haibun

"Dog," she says a propos of nothing, pointing a chubby, accusing finger at the dog, lounging innocently on the settee. We take her outside at dusk for a breath of fresh air after a hot summer's day, just the hour when the moon rises over the field very full and white.

"Moon," we tell her.

"Moo," she cries, lilting the word. Over and over she chants, lowing like a little calf. Ever after, on dark nights of the new moon, she scans the sky perturbed, demanding the miracle of the glowing orb of light. One day soon I will tell her about the Apollo 11 landing conversation, will tell her about Chang'e and her Chinese rabbit, who are rumored to abide on the moon these 4,000 years.

"Just look there," I will say, "for the cinnamon tree under which he stands on hind legs, waiting for his mistress to come home." Those who worship the beauty of the moon, I will tell her, are beautiful in return. And perhaps I will not have to tell her anything at all. Perhaps she will tell me.

> the show goes on
> moon rises
> takes its bow

The Poet Updates Israfel

"None sing so wildly well/ As the angel Israfel."
—EDGAR ALLAN POE

Above the orbit
Makes low its music—
Acting agent of the stars.

To threaten & steal & dice
An unknown immorality
As Poe said somewhat:

Easier to sing solemn
The pure green good
When you are vanilla

Perfection without salt
To uncheck thy bliss,
But this,

Israfeli, is a weaker world.

The Daughter

When I was a very little girl—*une toute petite fille*—
I would learn French, I would. Conjunctive, consumptive,
fat yet frail, mousy, serious browed-thing, cher Papa: teach me.

My papa was not a rolling stone who gathers no moss.
He was a rolling stone who gathered speed and took
his earthly goods along with him. My first lesson: the inertia to flee.

He did love us, my mother swears. *Why, once* when I was one and
tottered to him, mute and obeisant, so desperate for him
I would cry tears mythic in their outpouring, endless, Sisyphean

tears, *pour toi, Papa.* You gave me Babar books before I could read.
I declared myself *le roi* that day on the crest of the world,
when my tricycle took the breeze and bore me into flight,

down the hill. You didn't care for such a brazen bit of DNA
spliced from you and her—a Jew. I was half you and learned
my Ah, Bay, Says and hated half my self. As you wished.

At lunch, those intervening years forgot, so grown up we were.
No more tears. No slaps, slammed phones, stony ears. No recriminations.
Polite on Park Avenue at your club, where I wore white without a slip.

"What a slip that is!" You sneered and made me take the servant's stairs.
After a lunch of salad *niçoise* and *café au lait* and your general
declarations of non-love: "I love you because you are my daughter,

and I *must*." I was no king Babar or any king. Half-naked in my thin
dress by the subway stairs, we paused to speak of it: how inappropriate it
was, my shoes, too. The blues. *Mais oui*...you told me I was your daughter

and you must love me as God does. Like you were God!
And how you loved humanity as a general thing en masse, like ants
you chose not to crush because your Sufi teacher once said:

"Life is in everything." I understood why Atheists loathe Him then.
To be loved as an ant. And those years I studied French, stifled
that half of me you, odious *Dieu*, cursed—the American, glowering
trop juive:

loud-laughing, left-fork holding side of me—when the truth is
(the truth!) you loved only your reflection in me. God who tells
Our sommelier I am his daughter not his date. He bows and says:

"I know, *monsieur*, she has your voice. You have the same voice."
Indeed. So listen when I speak Papa. *Mon amour. Mon
chagrin, mon passé, mon présent*—you are the half of me

I will obliterate. When our lunch came, it came a little too late.
The food was cold, gelid on the plate. Pour toi, Papa: I came, I
saw, by these same laws: *fraternité, égalité, liberté…*

Convenient catchwords, *mon situationiste, ex-anarchiste,
Park-Avenuiste* (how convenient creeds have been I see.)
Oh by all the gods, I agree: you have not, cannot conquer me

The Girl in the Ghetto Contemplates Life from Nowhere New Jersey

Blue air of summer is heaven
down to our ankles walking, shimmering
up Jersey Ave in a lake of the gods.
Julius, taking Greek this year at that private school, sings:
Hail Helios! in high noon mansion baking asphalt
black, new black, black as a scar of night,   *yeah cat, yeah,*
deep pain and absence of pain into the deep day. *snap, deep, so deep,*
We leave Jersey Ave with its intimations of heaven
and hell, take the footpath past a crabbed factory:

where birds have taken over *means of production:*
down with the man, man
here are birdbaths in the factory floor, nests in officium,
widow's weeds through busted window frames,
glass crushed on rock, like a union man's spectacles
dashed, but reeds, fumes sweeten together
around the canal bridge over the stagnant stream's
waters green and thick, a tongue of sludge
lapping the factory's corpse, rotting from the bad, old days.

Another hundred yards, pick our way to a world
of ships and sailors, of jackdaws, gander and gosling:
wherefore is a river clean and forgiving,
gray, tender blue, speckled with white-hot kisses of noon
sunlight. The City across the waters looks one
immense graveyard; high-rises heavy, squat as tombs,
somber, glowering city, mirage of stillness, caesura.
By docked, dry rot rowboats we lunch, watching the waters

wash the dead heart in the reeds, lap up against
driftwood weeds to carry the sulphurous salt
to the wide, calling sea; there by the old ships
do we lounge all afternoon, we do, *wedo, wedooo...   do we? dowe dowe do*
where nests are built sharp, grassy among flaking hulls,
corrosions of boat and factory, among thorns and wet trash
by brown Hudson waters rose waters
gray waters ashen water dusk and navy, high noon.

Festering, old canal mouth, your putrescent nests
call at sundown: Home! Home! Flying from the sea
one black arrow, becomes ten, separate arrows, swift
falling above us, arcing clean in Nyx's twilight throttle,   *says Julius before*
he kisses me oh gods, old gods! At night the dead city alive

glows jewel-bright, now a necklace displayed
on the pale neck of sky, on alpine-glow
of mountain-hued rock revealing origins

of the silent-seeming city, red as mountain tops.
Julius sings. He is my king.
What does it mean for us, children of Nowhere New Jersey,
when there is so much beauty in decay?
So much beauty in the dusk, the death of the day,
the broken walls of mountainsides, the filthy, brown
lagoon above which we sat and talked of our already
defeated lives, of our already spent dreams. *Julius kissed me. Julius did.*
I am his Romeo. He is my Julius.
Across the water, we watch them live. We
have forgotten what it means to talk together, to hope
for a revolution, of another world, but moments like
these we do dream together, we do *wedo wedo*. *Tonight I am not afraid.*

The Manga Girl Imagines Her Creator

There is a ragged teen angel reading
Manga in the alleyway, back behind the skateboard shop.

 Soon his apocalyptic visions of large-eyed
Nymphs cavorting with white hands

Signaling like semaphores the recurring message
Of surrender will spread forth,

An army of avant-garde consumers,
Uniting at last *l'artiste, le savant et l'industriel*.

She wears a blue dress and she waits
Patiently for him by the window in Paterson.

There is a halo upon her,
Imagined or real slant of sun. His supper is

Cooked tomatoes, a hock of ham, green beans
From the garden, but he has read Rimbaud ("I is another")

And watches electric lights go bright in Tompkins Square
Park where nightly the saxophonist plays

"Somewhere Over the Rainbow", not hoping for utopia
But quarters, crumpled dollar bills.

He has come from that other land,
From the rainbow's end; he is here to report,

Spreading word by skateboard by land, swimming the East River
And avoiding the tugging tides of the nearby sea so dim and salty

On the horizon, over which an F train under the moon speeds.
There is nothing really to report.

All April the white pear blossoms quivered
On 9th Street and fell unseen until one day

They were dirty confetti like gray snow two days
After the storm, tracing designs of ash, just another whimsical

Drawing in the dust like a mandala, a spark stamped out
("…every sun bitter"). Beautiful then—

Poof… a vanished dream, like me.
We are all hoping for so much more.

The Eternal Grandmother, or The Supreme Moment Is Now

1. Now, my mother's hair is white
2. Now, my mother bends slowly from her hips
3. Now, she bends slowly to pluck the violet from the path
4. My mother is acaulescent, like the humble, heart-shaped flower
5. Acaulescent is a botanical term and means to have no stem
6. Or to appear not to have a stem
7. Appearances are deceiving
8. From the earth, my mother seems to spring complete, like Athena from her father's skull
9. My mother with her white hair seems to be the eternal grandmother from birth
10. With hair so white and pure like undyed silk, it never had corrupting color, no, nor never could
11. Evenings we walk, my mother and I, passing gardens, garbage cans, pre-fab playgrounds
12. The playgrounds are acaulescent, too, appearing almost overnight, useless weeds in a row of houses tinged gray-blue by time and sultry shadow
13. There are no children to play anymore in the acaulescent playgrounds
14. The swings float empty in the wind
15. The swings remind me of ravens' wings, a ragged fluttering on the edge of eyes, ravaging the soul, an ill omen, fluttering nerveless
16. The swings are the only movement and pull focus
17. The swings hedge these staggering rows of identical houses a Blaue Reiter painter would have painted as a patchwork quilt on an angry ochre sky
18. Behind, in the shadows, there are patches of forest so green they burn black
19. This forest is nothing like the Schwarzwald's velvet black whose nap of darkness has been rubbed the wrong way by evil hands
20. This forest is small, young, even its shadows are dappled with light
21. On the edges of the forest the saplings are thin as twisted fingers yet beckon like the wizened hand of witches or an old king of legend
22. *Come into the portal of the shadowed day, where the secrets of the juniper, the bald cypress, the river birch are fed from the smoky waters where leaping, darting fish abide*
23. When I was small in the world, I would trawl the stream
24. I would explore every inch of this margin of woods, this pale sliver of soil and tree
25. The copse seemed vast as a Biblical kingdom, vast as Persia, as Alexander's world
26. I was always searching for lost spectacles, pennies, Indian arrowheads

27. I never found any of the above.
28. I did find once a diamond ring with three small diamonds like very small wishes, granted by a mean genie
29. I never again find so much as a four-leafed clover, though we tread the path until my mother's hair turns soft and white, a cloud or nimbus around her head
30. The houses, too, are paler, washed out, more gray than blue
31. At night, even the stars seem paler, washed out, more gray than white
32. Above, the shining stars sullenly proclaim nighttime with the cold, clear insistence of a car alarm, as if there is no day, no peace
33. As if there never was
34. Hovering at the edge of the world are beautiful monsters in dreams
35. Inside, my mother's pale blue house I must cling to the couch, as if I might fall into that coruscating abyss of glitter and desolation
36. One day in the mirror, I have silver in my hair and a flash of gold hurts my eyes
37. The flash of gold is sunlight in the mornings, reflected from the silver mirror, although I cannot be certain.
38. I take pills, I am prone to colds
39. "Oh little children," the leaves whisper, always with no sense of kairos
40. The time is not right
41. The time will never be right again
42. The supreme moment is now
43. But we don't mind, my mother who is dead does not mind
44. I am my mother, and she was her mother
45. That is the secret of eternity
46. That is the essence of eternity, that is the essence of a secret, that is what the kings and witches are saying even now in the fairy tales shut away
47. The supreme moment is now, that is all it adds up to 1-50 easy steps
48. Now, I pull the curtains close, because the air is so bright a blue
49. Now, I must rest more often and tell myself to remember
50. Now, I must remember what I sometimes dreamed the violin sang, sawing through branch and wind

The Dreamer

I dreamed of the wide lake again whose
blue, unruffled depths conceal the monster.
This dream of the off-stage king has
obsessed my nights although by day I am
indolent, often unkind, of a savage temper
not easily ruled or subdued—
even by myself.

I little imagine how my prince could come
to be devoured by my local tribe who see
the gilded lily of his pretty cap, the bejeweled
tunics of his pretty men as invitations to feast on flesh—
royal and raw though it is. Inside me, I am savage.
The princes and ships and kings I dream of are
bloody conquerors anyway. Not romantic leads.

I hate and long for them.

And once I dreamed I was both the girl the boys chased
and one boy himself. All in cotton-white brave with curled
hair and short trousers and lordly soft kid boots.
How we tussled in the wave, half-dying until the rough,
lapping water subdued the band. And again female, solitary
like a slimy, slippery fish I made my escape.

Half-drowned I awoke

on the top of the sea above the gold-lit depths,
floating on a paltry, pitiful raft beside a poor fisherman
who whispered a name that was never mine again
or since: *his Shulamith*. But I was black-haired
in the dream and not myself, and it was voluptuous and sincere
how I loved that lonely fisherman and lived with him

and only dreamed of absent monsters and invisible kings.

The Hipster Loves

> "*I remember you well from the Chelsea Hotel/ And that's all. I don't think of you that often.*"   LEONARD COHEN

As the song goes, "I remember you well." And yet, I'm not lovelorn.
In the day, I don't love you or long for you. There were days upon

days I ached from the hairs on my head unto heels
I'd imagine cracking from the weight of gathered steps,

wearing and wearying the bare boards nightly like a ghost
haunted with love, like that old, familiar cliché of love.

That's all done. I won't bore you with reminiscences
that bore even me—I've grown up, learned irony good as wisdom.

But at night there remains within me an unhip place I can't reach
Like a country cut off from diplomatic missions

That sometimes dreams of you, living again those summer
Days I waited for your raspy voice, your laugh, your satirical

unease to reach me through a thin wire or the sun and earth's diurnal
duet meant nothing but a series of wobbly oscillations, baking me slowly

like meat rotating on a spit. Though we never said much,
conscious of a great, rotating continent between us. Then, over time,

that other distance formed, proper nouns replaced the intimate, only
pronoun: you. But all that was years ago.

I don't even think about you. Or when I do it's not with love.
Still, at night I dream of you, as if there is a spot inside

me permanently marked with an afterglow of hope,
so that perhaps the soul's ghostly footsteps, pacing through

my echoing skull, from time to time in dreams pass so near
the signpost, signifying where once a wild civilization subsisted

and there recognize the sunken city, summon its custom and languages
to being again, dust off the soot over a spot where once rose a vast

monument to love, now crumbled, another foolish Ozymandias
vanished, forgotten, except for this invisible scar, a narcissistic indentation

upon either side of which, on opposite banks, two strangers sit,
while perhaps only one acknowledges the fissure for what it is:

a buried ruin in the land of dreams where myth reigns
and our clichéd romance sometimes through the surreal work of dreams

becomes a great story of love.

The Student

I'm waiting for you on a bench outside the tea lounge with the dog. There are children everywhere, because this is Brooklyn and across the way is an all-natural frozen fruit ice cream parlor. I see a balloon, floating free from the shadows and up into the light, crawling up the side of a brownstone like a spider then floating across the roofs, where it darkens from white to pale gray in the open sky like a tiny storm cloud. It's banal but beautiful.

"Excuse me. Who has lost their balloon?"

A little girl pushes her scooter. She's wearing a pink safety helmet and one day she'll be lovely. She's speaking to me, I realize. "It's all right," I say. "It was beautiful." I offer her the banality with the word, and she shakes her head, unsatisfied with my insipidity. Her father tries to apologize.

"But someone lost that balloon," she insists. Concern furrows her small brow. I pick out a smiling boy across the way and point.

"He did, see? But he doesn't mind."

She nods.

"That's all right then."

"Come along," her father says, grimacing apologetically.

"Wait!" Her eyes meet mine. "What's your name then?"

It's of vital importance I don't smile. I tell her.

"What's yours?" I say.

"Reese," she tells me, and, slowly, she repeats mine.

She looks at me with eyes grave and sweet like yours, and I just love her.

"Good-bye, Izzy," she says gravely, sweetly.

"Good-bye, Reese."

She floats away, her father's hand barely holding her to the Earth.

The Historian

If you read an Egyptian love poem,
the worm ourbouros might bite you.
You'll see.
Eternal return—that bitch,
as Nietzsche somewhat said,
railing against *amor fati*.

Proof even a philosopher
couldn't think his way out of the bitterness
of biology we've prettied up as love.

Read an Egyptian "pleasant song", you'll learn
the worst, find out we're destined
to live the same lie forever.
Nothing
has changed at all.

Your voice gives life, like nectar.

It's terrible. Such lies. We've had millennia to think
but most of us
still mooning over The One.

"Setting our hair and curling it"
when it doesn't turn out just right.
Setting our trap for the next.

We walked in the garden of trees,
indeed. I will not be the one to bathe the dust
from your feet. You can forget that.
Turn on the tap. That's progress, I suppose.

This could be Cairo or the
Great Desert if it existed then—
sand for miles like my heart
after you seared it with all
those false promises.

My beloved is the best of medicine,
        Better than all pharmacopeia.

I knew those drugstore promises were
misleading as magazine ads,

showing the pretty, chemical ways
I could improve my chances with you.

Would I be better as Bottle Blonde?
In life, love, or laughter. No!
A thousand life-times, no!
Essential me is platonic Brunette,
unchangeable as Euclid's geometry,
abjuring biochemical cunning.

That seems like progress
of a kind. More *amour-propre* than the
other. *Fati*. Fate.

God knows you never told me
odes to my hands and breasts
as he did that lover crumbled
to dust who seduces me yet.

"Darling, you only, there is no
duplicate." History says not so.
But there's no irony
in these lines, no comfortable space.

I never said, "When you embrace
me so bright is the light that shines
from you, I need balm for my eyes."

But I felt it.
My manners were too
good to demand more of you than
you gave. And I too gave only measured,
equal shares: drop of love per drop.

A democratic love for a democratic age.

Still.

Your face really was like a snare in the forest
of *meryu*, (whatever that is you may well ask).

Oh God, it was.
It really was.

Just so you know.

"La Sérieuse" Academic Lectures

There is so much talk of blue plums,
So I went to the market. Bought them.
Bought an old wheelbarrow, too. Used. Chipped.
Painted it red, then sprayed it with my garden hose

To achieve the raindrops. An old garden hose arcing through
The hazy summer air, glittering droplets of sunlight,
Diffuse as Greek verbs whose accents haunt my sleeping hours still.
Tin andra, tin eroa, tina theon means approximately

As much as the printed images on a porcelain plate
Or ukiyo-e prints on rice paper.
So fragile, so evanescent are we a whole world can vanish
Easily as a shattered plate upon the floor. Burn up into the moon.

A flash of light and all is gone.
We take our *petits morts* far too personally,
But somehow brittle and hard, too, as the
Varnish of scarlet paint that's been our image of the rose.

That crimson I could scrape from young minds even easier
Than from a rock. Scrape clean. Blank as a face in the crowd.
A double-banksia rose at that. Such a lovely name from
Which little is expected, a resistance to aphids and thrips

And unpoetic rose slugs. We must remember to fear
The real day the bumblebee's buzz ceases to be like the rain,
An ordinary miracle. My heroes, my gods, my kings:
where have you gone? To save us, sleeping under the roses

Of reification for now. In the modern jargon,
you can never be one and the same: ideal and real.
Fighters or dreamers. Who wears our wreath?
Who will be our just, hospitable Bulwark of Agrigentum?

(Forgive these sentimental tears. I've forgotten the old thread.)
Who will save the roses? Who will save the bees? Not I.
Will you ask yourselves why "what I like to drink most is wine
That belongs to others."

Generally, you see, this is why I ask no questions
That can't be answered.

Easily.

The Sisters: A Haibun

Highway 70 climbs across America to the Rockies. My sister and I check off Indiana, Kansas, Missouri in our ascent. We battle a Hades-hot sun. The highway shimmers. The heartland of America burns through the windshield, wipes the dog out, turns our thighs rosy; chests blush as if Apollo himself were making love to us. We endure for the sake of a higher goal: Colorado and the house my sister's selling.

Near Limon we pause to stretch. The dog's frisky again in the cool, clear air. To us the change betokens nearness to the peaks' perfection. But Kansas City, St. Louis, all that farmland between is beautiful to somebody. And beautiful too the muggy lowlands, the clinging green which goes to feed the cattle peopling these high fields with their cheerful bovine faces, so different from those miles of Midwest cornfields. Emptiness for us to pass through to another is the heartbeat of a nation.

Past Limon we see a stand of cottonwoods planted, or so my sister says, as shade for cattle. She's a professor now and states opinions as facts. A calf nuzzles its mother.

"I'll never eat beef again," I say. My sister snorts. The back of her fuel-efficient car is filled with my forbidden bottles. I wouldn't drink from the hotel taps. As if like Persephone I could enchant myself into a trap. My sister just says, "Never mind beef. The real evil is plastic bottles."

And then the road opens up; the faint mirage that might have been a distant city becomes jagged, substantial, real– the hunched shoulders of those old rocks meditating like some great old Zen master of the past bringing the questioners peace. Our arguments cease.

> sky lightens
> over horsetooth peak
> the sparrows watch

After Happily Ever After

Eventually Princess
Has to grow up. Then what?
Either she bears his children, grows fat,

A double chin, skin tags,
Varicose veins like lines in blue cheese.
The catafalque of too-fragrant flesh

She must carry around,
Betting on his gratitude
A memory of once lustrous eyes,

Cheeks velvet as peonies, lips dipped
In blood, though she has learned
To dread scarlet, gushing as it did

Until she prayed to die,
Cut open like a melon
So he might have his princey,

But only another useless bint
Upon the lacy sheet, congeries of shes, condemned
By birth to play the princess again. Again.

Is it any wonder Stepmother
From her oriel window
Was made distraught by sight of that eternal
She in the pleasaunce with her gold ball:

Insensate, disordered, so unkind—
Who's to say who the true villain is?
No wonder that Other lost her mind,

That basket of apples ripe at her feet.
Oh the mocking fountains—
A diuturnity of plashing tears.

Silver as that mirror she gazes into
Now. It would be well to be a witch,
Free of this sinister envy

In the subfusc forest, shadows dance,
Twirl about as once she did on those
Slippered feet until they were shreds,

Ribbons and toes alike.
What did she care hearing the
Shawms play contrapuntal harmony?

Another song keens forth now,
Not so jocund as the gold day
Echoed in the clear blue bowl of sky,

Muted by the arch of Palladian elm, oak,
And the wild eglantine. A sea mist
Before her obscures the field of asphodel

She climbs,
Panting, not so lissome as once was
Upon that time,

Circling the tarn on the mountaintop,
Gazing into serene pools,
Worn, wrinkled, but sure-footed still

She grins. The simple relief. The daws
Croak, cackle in wicked companionship,
The day goes down,

Now at last,
In the obscurity of starlight,
She can tap, sing, live, croon, wreathing reveries

Into a soul less sinister
Than that painted sheet they
Adorned with pearls and called a person.

www.ingramcontent.com/pod-product-compliance
Lightning Source LLC
Chambersburg PA
CBHW060224050426
42446CB00013B/3161